Creepy - Crawlies Are Fun

Moira Andrew

Illustrated by Alexandra Maslova

Printed in the United States of America

A 2 Z Press LLC

PO Box 582

Deleon Springs, FL 32130

bestlittleonlinebookstore.com

sizemore3630@aol.com

440-241-3126

ISBN: 978-1-954191-64-8

Dedication

For Erin,
Genevieve, Joe,
Sam, & Harry

This book belongs to :

_____

I like every kind of insect.

I like the ones that crawl.

I like the ones that tickle me,

And those that are very small.

I like the insects that dance,

And those that flutter in the air.

I like the ones that hop about,

And those all covered with hair.

I like the beetles that twist -

To show off shiny black backs,

I like the ones that slip along.

Leaving slippery silver tracks,

I like the insects that jump –

I like the ones that squiggle,

I like the insects that loop-the-loop,

and those that squirm and wriggle.

I like the insects
that buzz,

And even those

that sting!

I like wasps and honey bees,

And those that fly
on the wing.

I'm not so sure
about mosquitoes,

And other insects that bite,

I love the fiery fireflies,

And the way they light up the night.

I like the insects that scutter,

And the ones that
swoop and glide.

I like spiders that make sticky webs,

And I like shy insects
that hide.

I like curly creepy-crawlies,

I like the ones that squirm,

those that make a figure-of-eight,

And I'm mad about the worm.

I love every creepy-crawlie,
    Indeed I love, love them all.

The End

Moira Andrew is a travelling poet and children's author who was born and educated in Scotland. She has worked in most areas of primary education as a teacher, head teacher, and college lecturer.

Moira taught creative writing part-time at the University of Glamorgan. She has written seven books on the creative arts for teachers, (Belair). She also writes stories and poems for children, *Wish a Wish*, (Poetry Space), is the most recent. She has tens of poetry collections for adults in publication, *Geese and Daughters* (IDP) and *Imagine a Kiss*, (Dempsey & Windle) are her most recent. Moira also has a very special book, *Looking through Water*, (Poetry Space) - *a sensitive and thoughtful* collection of poetry documenting her failing sight that is being recorded by the RNIB as a Talking Book for the blind.

Moira has over 100 titles and
more than 2500 poems to her credit!

Some Other Books
by Moira Andrew

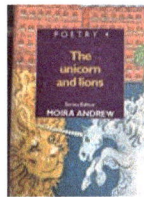

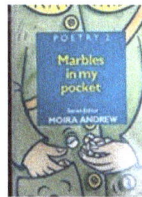

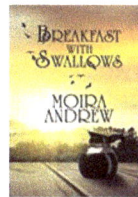

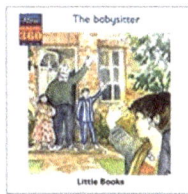

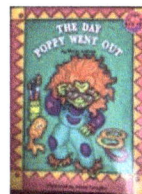

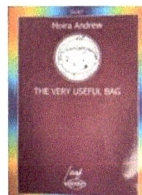

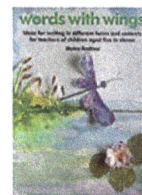

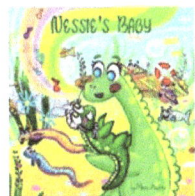

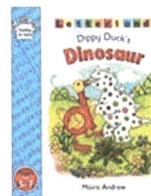

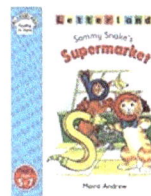

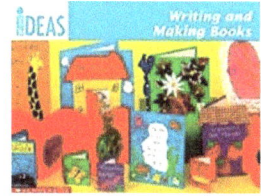

And many, many more to come!

In 1989 Moira Andrew, then the head of a primary school in Bristol, UK, was sorting the mail. She found a flyer from a new publisher called Belair. She found it very interesting; all the subjects covered except for Creative Writing, Poetry, and Art!

A few weeks later, the first of her books "Language in Colour" was contracted! In the 1990's-2000's, these books for teachers were in every school in the UK. Moira became a full time writer. Many teachers that she knows still have their personal copies.

Unfortunately, they are long out of print as the curriculum has changed. It became much more prescriptive, and creativity discouraged! What a waste! (Though you can still find copies if you go on line.)

Moira wrote most weeks for the teachers' magazine, 'Child Education' (Scholastic) and often her poetry appeared as Posters for the classroom wall. Here are the covers of the complete set. They are brim full of creative ideas, lesson plans, children's work, and suggestions for display. Still writing every day, she has 101 books to her name and there are currently 5 more being published! Moira is a remarkable woman!

Samples of Moira's Lovely Poster Poems

(Scholastic)

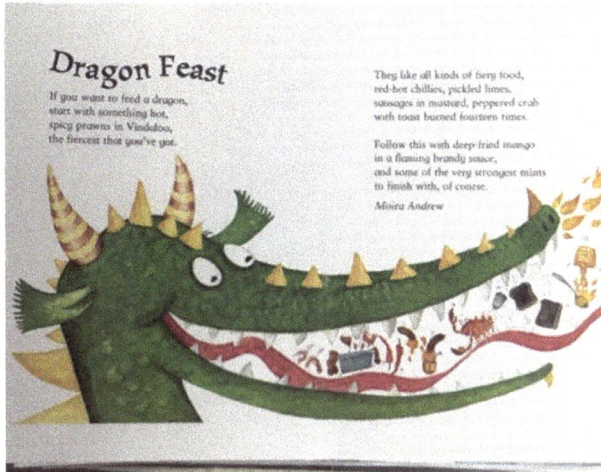

Dragon Feast

If you want to feed a dragon,
start with something hot,
spicy prawns in Vindaloo,
the fiercest that you've got.

They like all kinds of fiery food,
red-hot chillies, pickled limes,
sausages in mustard, peppered crab
with toast burned fourteen times.

Follow this with deep-fried mango
in a flaming brandy sauce,
and some of the very strongest mints
to finish with, of course.

Moira Andrew

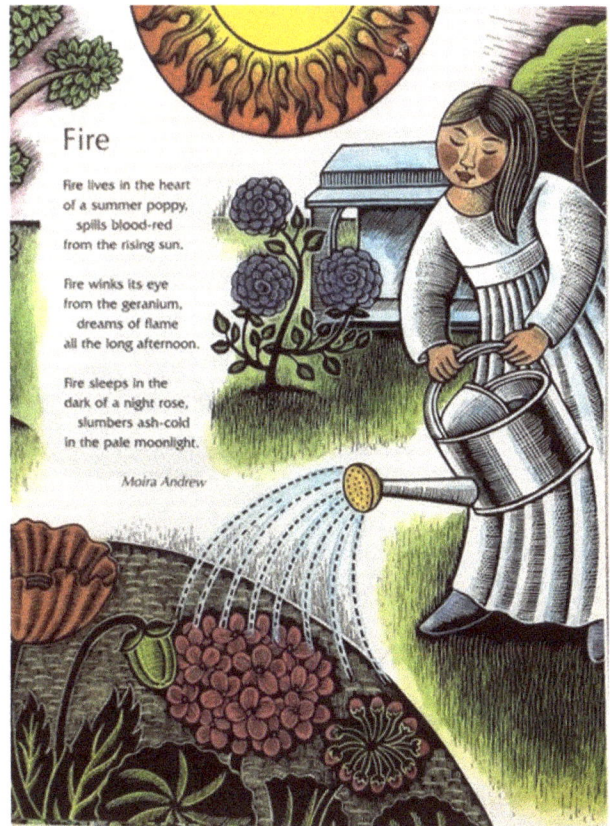

Fire

Fire lives in the heart
of a summer poppy,
  spills blood-red
from the rising sun.

Fire winks its eye
from the geranium,
  dreams of flame
all the long afternoon.

Fire sleeps in the
dark of a night rose,
  slumbers ash-cold
in the pale moonlight.

Moira Andrew

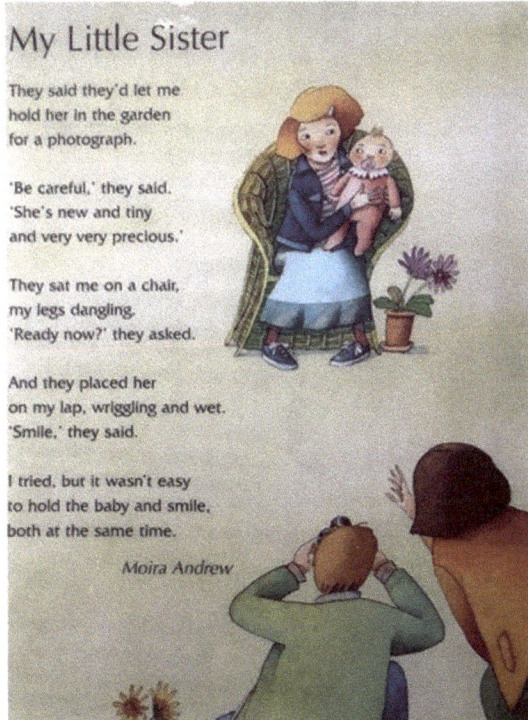

My Little Sister

They said they'd let me
hold her in the garden
for a photograph.

'Be careful,' they said.
'She's new and tiny
and very very precious.'

They sat me on a chair,
my legs dangling.
'Ready now?' they asked.

And they placed her
on my lap, wriggling and wet.
'Smile,' they said.

I tried, but it wasn't easy
to hold the baby and smile,
both at the same time.

Moira Andrew

Visit Moira's Website

Visit www.moiraandrew.com for

all the latest titles and

more information about Moira!

www.ingramcontent.com/pod-product-compliance
Lightning Source LLC
Chambersburg PA
CBHW042333030426
42335CB00027B/3326